THE USBORNE BOOK OF
ANIMAL
FACTS

W9-ABC-093

Anita Ganeri

CONTENTS

Illustrated by Tony Gibson and Ian Jackson

**Additional illustrations by
Pam Corfield**

**Designed by Tony Gibson
and Steve Page**

**Consultant: Michael Boorer,
Education Officer, London Zoo**

What is a mammal?

How many mammals?

There are over 4,000 different kinds of mammals in the world. These are divided into 19 groups called 'orders'. The rodent order is the biggest with about 1,750 species, while the aardvark is the only living member of its order. There are very few mammals in the world compared to other animals and there are hundreds of times more insects than there are mammals.

DID YOU KNOW?

All mammals breathe air. The distant ancestors of mammals were fish and mammals still have some traces of gills for breathing underwater. The tube running between a mammal's ear and its throat is really a gill-slit.

Central heating

Mammals are warm-blooded. This means that the temperature inside their bodies stays about the same . whatever the weather is like outside. Most mammals have a body temperature of about 36°C-39°C (97°F-102°F).

Warm blood allows mammals to be very active and to live in a wide variety of places, from the icy Poles to the hot Tropics. Fur and fat help protect them from the cold and they get rid of excess heat by sweating or panting.

Hair history

Mammals are the only animals with true hair. Hairs are dead cords of a substance called keratin which is also found in nails. What looks like hair on spiders and flies actually contains living parts of the animal. All mammals have some hair, though you would need a magnifying glass to see the fine hair on the lips of a young whale.

Backbones

Mammals are vertebrates which means that they all have backbones. Most of the animals in the world have no backbone. All mammals, except for some sea-cows and sloths, have seven bones in their necks. This includes giraffes whose necks can be 2 m (6½ ft) long and mice who seem to have no neck at all.

The kinds of living mammals

Family	Examples	Number of species
Rodents	Rats, mice, squirrels, porcupines	about 1,750
Chiropterans	Bats	about 950
Insectivores (insect eaters)	Shrews, hedgehogs	300
Carnivores (meat eaters)	Dogs, cats, bears, weasels	about 250
Marsupials (pouched mammals)	Kangaroos, possums	about 240
Primates	Bush babies, monkeys, apes	about 180
Ungulates (even-toed)	Cattle, deer, hippos, pigs	about 180
Cetaceans	Whales and dolphins	about 85
Lagomorphs	Rabbits and hares	about 60
Pinnipedes	Seals, sealions, walruses	32
Edentates	Armadillos, sloths, giant anteaters	about 30
Ungulates (odd-toed)	Tapirs, rhinos, horses	15
Pangolins	Scaly anteaters	7
Monotremes (egg layers)	Platypus, spiny anteaters	6
Hyraxes		6
Sirenians	Sea cows and manatees	4
Dermopterans	Flying lemurs	2
Elephants		2
Aardvark		1

Care for the young

All mammals look after their young and feed them on milk. They are the only animals that produce milk. The length of time a baby is looked after by its parents varies from a few weeks for mice to several years for apes.

Earflaps

Mammals are the only animals with flaps around their ears. These direct sound down into the ears. Some sea and burrowing mammals have lost their earflaps as they have become adapted for life in the water or underground.

Poison

Only two types of mammal are poisonous. Some shrews have a slightly poisonous bite. Male platypuses have poisonous spurs on their back legs.

3

The first mammals

Reptile relations

About 250 million years ago most land animals were reptiles. About 200 million years ago some began to develop into mammals. One of the earliest mammals, Megazostrodon, lived 190 million years ago in Africa. It was about 10 cm (4 in) long and looked like a shrew.

Mammals on the move

At the time when the dinosaurs died out, 65 million years ago, mammals began to develop more fully into the three main groups we have today:

Monotremes are those mammals which lay eggs such as the duck-billed platypus.

Marsupials are mammals with pouches. They give birth to tiny babies which crawl into the mother's pouch to feed on milk until they are fully developed.

Placental mammals are the largest group. The baby grows and is nourished inside the mother's body until it is born.

Prehistoric pouches

Millions of years ago, two kinds of giant marsupials lived in Australia. Procoptodon was a huge kangaroo, about 3 m (10 ft) tall, twice the height of a modern kangaroo. Diprotodon was a giant wombat and the largest marsupial ever. It weighed as much as a hippopotamus.

Horse race

The first horses lived about 55 million years ago in the North American forests. Hyracotherium was only the size of a fox and had toes on its feet. Horses grew bigger and developed hooves so they could run faster. Equus, the modern horse, first lived about 2 million years ago.

Super sloth

Megatherium was a type of giant sloth which lived about 15,000 years ago. It was as high as a modern elephant and over 6 m (19 ft) in length. Today's sloths are about a tenth of its size.

First diets

Most early mammals ate insects and worms. Carnivores or meat-eaters first lived about 35 million years ago. The largest carnivore ever lived 20 million years ago. Megistotherium was bigger than a grizzly bear. It attacked and killed huge elephants. One of the fiercest carnivores was Smilodon, the sabre-toothed tiger. It had long pointed teeth for tearing meat apart.

Amazing But True

The first elephants lived 40 million years ago. Moeritherium was only as big as a large pig and had no tusks or trunk. Today's African elephant is 300 times bigger. Deinotherium, which lived 15 million years ago, was much larger than today's elephants. It had tusks which curved back towards its chest. It probably used them like forks to dig up food.

Thunder beast

The giant mammal, Brontotherium, or 'thunder beast', lived 35 million years ago in North America. It was about the size of a hippo and had a forked horn on the end of its nose, perhaps for fending off enemies. This huge creature ate only leaves and fruit.

Little and large

The ancestors of today's camels lived about 10 million years ago. Unlike modern camels, they had no humps. Stenomylus was a tiny animal, only as big as a small door. Alticamelus was about 3 m (10 ft) tall, with long legs and a long neck, like a giraffe's, for reaching leaves high up in the trees.

Sea giant

A giant whale, Basilosaurus, was the largest prehistoric sea mammal. It was more than 20 m (65 ft) long, about 7 m (13 ft) smaller than a blue whale, the largest sea mammal alive today. It lived 40 million years ago.

Baby mammals

Tail first

The biggest animal baby is a blue whale calf. Unlike most mammals, whales and dolphins are born tail first. Because it is born underwater, the baby has to be pushed quickly to the surface by its mother so that it can breathe. A new-born calf can only stay underwater for about 30 seconds at a time.

Marsupial mother

When a baby kangaroo, or 'joey', is born it is only about the size of a bee and is blind and helpless. The joey crawls into its mother's pouch and stays there for six months, feeding on milk and growing. It comes out of the pouch for the first time after about 28 weeks and leaves the pouch for good after about 33 weeks.

Smallest babies

The smallest mammal babies are probably those of the mouse opossums in Central and South America. The new-born babies of some species are only as big as grains of rice.

Who am I?

An elephant in the Kruger National Park South Africa chose its own family and now thinks it is a buffalo. It was brought to the park in the 1970s with four other elephants to live near a herd of buffalo.

This elephant soon joined the herd and was accepted as being part of it. It was seen by park rangers drinking from a waterhole with its new buffalo 'family' and running off when a herd of elephants came near.

Egg layer

When the duck-billed platypus was discovered in 1797 people thought that it must be either a duck or a reptile because it was found to lay eggs. The female builds her nest in a river bank tunnel and in it lays soft, sticky eggs. But when the babies hatch they feed on their mother's milk showing that the platypus is in fact a mammal, although a very strange one.

Mammals and their babies

Mammal	Average pregnancy	Usual number of young
Asian elephant	20 months	1
Indian rhinoceros	18 months	1
Giraffe	15 months	1
Blue whale	11 months	1
Human being	9 months	1
Chimpanzee	8 months	1
Dog	2 months	3-6
Red kangaroo	35 days	1
House mouse	19 days	4-32
American opossum	13 days	10

Most babies

The mammal which has the most young is the common vole. It can have its first litter when it is only 15 days old and has 4-9 babies as often as 15 times a year. In her lifetime, a female vole may have 33 litters, a total of as many as 147 young.

Growing up fast

The striped tenrec in Madagascar is the mammal which grows up the fastest. Two babies born in Berlin Zoo in July 1961 could run almost at once and eat worms by the age of six days. Other mammals can still only drink their mother's milk at this age.

Longest pregnancy

The mammal which has the longest pregnancy (called the gestation period) is an Asian elephant. The pregnancy lasts for 20-22 months, 33 times as long as that of a house mouse. Another female elephant from the herd who is called the 'auntie' helps look after the new baby.

Shortest pregnancy

An American opossum has a pregnancy of only 12-14 days and it may even be as short as eight days. The babies, though, still need to spend another 10 weeks feeding in their mother's pouch before they are fully developed.

Amazing But True

The nine-banded armadillo gives birth to sets of identical quads. Most mammals have babies which look different and are of different sexes. Armadillo quads are always identical and always of the same sex.

Mammal lives

Grand old age

The mammal which lives the longest, after man, is the Asian elephant. The oldest on record was called Modoc. She died in California, USA in July 1975, at the age of 75. During her long career in the circus, Modoc survived two attempts to poison her and a terrible fire. The fire made her a heroine when she dragged the lions' cage out of the big top tent to safety. She starred in several TV series before retiring.

Sea life

Baird's beaked whale is the longest–living sea mammal known. It can live for up to a maximum of about 70 years.

The oldest ape was a male orang-utan called Guas in the Philadelphia Zoo, USA. He died in 1977 at the age of 57. Massa, an African western lowland gorilla from the same zoo, celebrated his 50th birthday in 1980. One of his presents was a T-shirt from the actor Clint Eastwood. Massa died in 1984.

Oldest horse

The oldest known horse was born in 1760 and died at the age of 62 in Lancashire, Britain. He spent most of his long life towing barges along the canals before he was retired to a farm in 1819. Horses are usually expected to live for about 25-30 years.

Ancient Nero

Nero, a lion in the Cologne Zoo, West Germany, died at the age of 29 in May 1907. This made him the longest-lived big cat. In the wild lions grow more slowly than in zoos. They usually live for 12-14 years and rarely for 20 years. The oldest tiger was an Indian tigress in the Adelaide Zoo, Australia who lived for 26 years and 3 months.

Life on the wing

Bats normally live for 10-20 years. The oldest bat known is an Indian flying fox. It died at London Zoo at the age of 31 years and 5 months.

Amazing But True

Lemmings are small, hamster-like rodents from Norway. Their lives seem to go in strange four year cycles. For the first three years the lemmings breed at an ever-increasing rate. Then they seem to panic at the overcrowding and leave their homes in millions to find more space. Their mad rush carries them until they reach rivers or the sea. Even then they plunge in and try to swim across but most drown.

Mammal life-spans

Human being	60-80 years
Asian elephant	70-75 years
Killer whale	50-70 years
Rhinoceros	20-50 years
Hippopotamus	40-50 years
Arabian camel	25-40 years
Chimpanzee	30-40 years
Bottle-nosed dolphin	25-40 years
Zebra	20-30 years
Red deer	Up to 20 years
Giraffe	15-25 years
Koala	15-20 years
Grey kangaroo	15-20 years
Giant anteater	Up to 14 years
Two-toed sloth	8-12 years
European hedgehog	6 years
European rabbit	Up to 5 years
Armadillo	4 years
Rat	4 years
Mole	3-4 years
Long-tailed shrew	12-18 months

Cats and dogs

Domestic cats usually live longer than dogs. The oldest cat was probably a tabby called Puss in Devon, Britain. She died in November 1937, one day after her 36th birthday. The oldest dog was an Australian cattle dog called Bluey who lived for 29 years and 5 months. Dogs usually live for about 8-15 years.

Shortest life

The tiny shrew has the shortest life-span of all the mammals. Most shrews live for only about 12-18 months in the wild. They are born one year, breed the next year and then die. The record life-span for a shrew in captivity is 2 years and 3 months.

What mammals eat

Regular meals

Because they are warm-blooded, mammals can be very active in both hot and cold weather. They need a lot of energy for hunting, finding homes and looking after their young. They get their energy from food and must eat regularly.

Amazing But True

The tiny Etruscan shrew has a giant appetite. An adult shrew weighs only 2 g (0.07 oz) but can eat up to three times its own weight in a day and cannot live for more than two hours without food. An adult human being would have to eat a sheep, 50 chickens, 60 large loaves and over 150 apples to match the shrew's meals.

Giant anteater

The South American giant anteater has a 60 cm (24 in) long tongue which it uses to catch ants – its staple diet. It tears open an anthill with its strong claws and pokes its sticky tongue around inside until it is coated with ants, then flicks it out and swallows the ants whole. It can do this twice a second and can easily catch well over 30,000 ants a day.

No drink

Koalas will only eat the leaves of five out of the 350 kinds of eucalyptus tree. The word 'koala' means 'no drink' in the Aborigine language and koalas almost never need to drink water, getting all the liquid they need from the leaves they eat.

Liquid diet

Vampire bats live on a diet of animal blood. They hunt at night and attack animals while they are asleep. The bat's saliva contains a substance which stops the blood from clotting and closing the wound. A great vampire bat weighs about 28 g (1 oz) and drinks about a tablespoonful of blood a day.

Excuse fingers

The aye-aye, a rare lemur in Madagascar, has long, thin middle fingers. It eats wood-boring insects. To catch them, the aye-aye knocks on the tree bark, listens for the insects to move, pokes its skewer-like finger inside and pulls them out.

Mammal diets

Mammal	Food
Rhinoceros	plants, leaves, grass
Fruit-bat	fruit, flowers, nectar
Gorilla	leaves, plants
Polar bear	seals, fish
Cheetah	antelopes, gazelles
Hedgehog	insects, worms
Tarsier	birds, lizards, insects
Long-tailed macaque	crabs, shell fish, fruit
Panda	bamboo, rats, snakes, flowers

Herbivore (plants)		Carnivore (meat)		Omnivore (both)	

Giant hunger

In spring and summer, a blue whale eats as much as four tonnes of food a day, about twice as much as a well-fed person eats in a year. It swims, mouth wide open, through the sea, sucking in thousands of litres of water which contains krill (tiny shrimp-like creatures). Instead of teeth, the whale has huge bony plates called baleen hanging down inside its mouth. They strain the water, leaving the krill.

High table

A giraffe's long neck allows it to reach its favourite food of leaves on branches up to 6 m (20 ft) off the ground. It uses its 40 cm (16 in) long tongue to grip and pull branches down so it can strip off the leaves with its rubbery lips.

DID YOU KNOW?

Elephants eat up to ½ tonne of plant food a day. They have 24 teeth for grinding it. The teeth do not grow all at once, but in fours. As the first set wears down, a second set grows. At the age of 45 an elephant grows its last teeth, each weighing 4 kg (9 lb).

Eyes, ears and noses

Super smell

Dogs have an excellent sense of smell. An Alsatian has 44 times more smell cells in its nose than a human being. It can smell things about one million times better than man. Dogs also have superb hearing. They can pick up much higher sounds than human ears are able to hear.

DID YOU KNOW?

In 1925 Sauer, a Dobermann Pinscher, tracked two thieves 160 km (100 miles) across the Great Karroo desert in South Africa just by following their scent.

Wide-eyed

The biggest mammal in the world, the blue whale, has the biggest eyes. They are as big as footballs, quite small for its huge size but over six times wider than a human eye and 150 times wider than a pygmy shrew's eyes.

What big eyes . . .

Animals that feed at night have special ways of finding their way in the dark. Some, such as moles and bats, have tiny eyes but very good hearing and smell. Others, such as bush babies and tarsiers, have huge-fronted eyes. The Eastern tarsier's eyes are 17 mm (0.6 in) across. If a human's eyes were the same size in proportion to its body, they would be as big as grapefruit.

Big ears

An African elephant has huge earflaps. Each is about 1.8 m (6 ft) across and nearly as big as a single bed sheet. Elephants flap their ears to keep cool and a female beats her ears on her back to call her young. An elephant spreads out its ears to make it look more threatening to enemies.

Ear conditioning

Ears get cold quickly especially if the wind is blowing. The jack rabbit from the USA and the fennec fox from the Sahara Desert use their huge ears to keep cool. Air blowing across the ears cools down the blood in the ears. The jack rabbit's ears can be 21 cm (8 in) long, a quarter of the total length of its body.

A duck-billed platypus has a beak similar to a bird's but it is soft. It uses its beak to sift mud for food and has a pair of nostrils near the tip. The beak has lots of very sensitive nerve endings and the platypus finds its food of worms and small fish by touch. Underwater, a platypus can cover its eyes and ears to stop water getting in.

Cats' eyes

At the back of a cat's eye there is a special layer which reflects light. This means that cats can make much better use of light than human beings. They can hunt well at night because they are able to see in very dim light.

Bat radar

Bats navigate and find food in the dark using sound. They make about 50 high squeaking noises a second. The sound hits a solid object and the bat's large sensitive ears pick up the echo. They seem to be able to tell the shape of an object by this echo.

In an experiment, bats used echo-location to fly through wires 30 cm (12 in) apart in total darkness without hitting them. If a bat's mouth is full it cannot squeak so some use their noses. Folds of skin called 'nose-leaves' around their noses direct sound like megaphones.

Star-nosed mole

Moles spend most of their lives underground searching for food. They have very poor eyesight but very sensitive noses. The star-nosed mole of North America has a strange rosette of 22 tentacles surrounding its nose. They help the mole find its way underground by touch.

Big nose

The African elephant has the biggest nose of any mammal. A large male's trunk is about 2.5 m (8 ft) from base to tip. The trunk is used for breathing, smelling and sucking up water. It also acts as an extra hand for picking up food and scratching. Elephants in Kenya's National Park even learnt to turn taps on with their trunks.

Tops and tails

Antlers and horns

Antlers are made of bone. They fall off every autumn and grow back in spring. Each year they get bigger and more branched. Usually only the males have antlers for fighting off rivals in the mating season. Horns are made of keratin which also makes hair. They grow throughout an animal's life.

Travellers' tails

A kangaroo uses its tail for balance. As it bounds along the ground, its body leans forward and its large tail is stretched out behind. In this way, a red kangaroo can leap over 7 m (25 ft) at a time, nearly four times the length of its body. Giant leaps of 12 m (40 ft) have been known.

Longest horns

The longest horns belong to the water buffalo in India. A huge bull shot in 1955 had horns which measured 4.24 m (14 ft) across from tip to tip.

Heavy headgear

The North American elk has the longest antlers of any animal. They can be up to 1.78 m (5.8 ft) long. The moose has the heaviest antlers. They can weigh as much as two heavy suitcases.

Amazing But True

Synthetoceras was a strange mammal which lived about 15 million years ago in North America. It looked like a deer but instead of antlers had two small horns on its forehead and a huge forked horn in the shape of a Y growing on its nose.

Getting the point

The white rhinoceros has a huge front horn. It can be up to 1.58 m (5 ft) long which is about three times as long as a human arm.

Rhinoceroses also have a shorter back horn. If the horns get broken off they will grow back at a rate of about ½ cm (¼ in) a month.

Secret weapon

The skunk's tail hides a very effective secret weapon. When it is threatened, the skunk lifts up its tail and squirts out a vile-smelling liquid from a gland hidden underneath. The terrible smell given off can reach up to ½ km (0.3 miles) away.

Useful tails

Squirrels make good use of their long, bushy tails. If they hibernate in winter they wrap their tails round them like fur coats to keep warm. The ground squirrel in the Kalahari Desert keeps cool by angling its tail over its head like a parasol.

Flying the flag

When ring-tailed lemurs are walking along the ground in search of food, each keeps its striped tail raised high in the air. This shows the others where each lemur is and keeps the group safely together.

Tree-top tails

Some mammals which spend their lives up in the tree-tops have 'prehensile' tails. This means the tail can be used as an extra arm or leg to grasp hold of the branches. Spider monkeys have such strong tails that they can easily support their whole body weight on their tail alone.

DID YOU KNOW?

The Asian elephant has the longest tail of any land mammal. Excluding the tuft of hair on the end, the tail can be up to 1.5 m (5 ft) long.

Mammal tails

Mammal	Body length	Tail length
Snow leopard	1.75 m	1.13 m
Jerboa	15 cm	30 cm
Red kangaroo	2 m	1.05 m
Giant anteater	1 m	60-90 cm
Long-tailed shrew	5-10 cm	3-8 cm
Spider monkey	40-62 cm	50-90 cm
Palm squirrel	11-18 cm	11-18 cm
Bottle-nosed dolphin	3-4 m	0.75 m (width)
Honey bear	1-1.2 m	5 cm
Hippopotamus	3-3.5 m	25-50 cm

Coats and camouflage

Warm coats

All mammals have some hair. It helps to keep them warm by stopping heat escaping from their bodies and helps protect them from injury. A mammal's coat usually has two sorts of hair – a soft underfur with longer 'guard hairs' on top. The colour of some coats helps hide the mammal from enemies and is also used for making signals.

Longest hair

Mammals that live in cold places have the longest hair. The musk ox in Greenland has hair 60-90 cm (24-35 in) long and can live in temperatures as low as −27°C (−60°F). Without its thick, warm coat it would freeze to death.

16

Hair flower

The hyrax has a very unusual hair 'flower'. On its back is a gland surrounded by long hairs of a different colour to its coat. When the hyrax is threatened these hairs stand on end so that the flower seems to 'bloom'.

Walrus whiskers

Some mammals have very sensitive whiskers which help them to find their way around in the dark or underwater. A walrus's moustache contains about 700 hairs. It uses these to feel its way around in murky water. The hairs may also be used as forks to hold shellfish in place while the walrus sucks out the soft insides.

Cunning colours

The patterned coats of mammals such as tapirs, tigers and giraffes help to hide them from enemies or to stalk their prey unnoticed. Their coats blend in with the patches of light and shadow in the jungles and grasslands where they live. The black and white coat of a Malayan tapir disguises it so well that, when it is lying on the forest floor, it looks like a harmless pile of stones.

Thick tufts

The tuft of hair at the end of an elephant's tail is about 20 cm (7½ in) long. Each hair can be up to 3 mm (0.1 in) thick, over 40 times thicker than human hair.

Hairy heirlooms

In the last Ice Age which ended 10,000 years ago, rhinoceroses and mammoths adapted to the freezing conditions by growing long, warm coats. Cave paintings show the woolly rhinoceros with a thick black and reddish coat. Whole mammoths have been found deep-frozen in the ground in Siberia with some of their coats still intact.

Pin cushion

Mammals' quills and prickles are types of hair but may be very hard and sharp. Some porcupines have quills up to 40 cm (16 in) long. A Canadian porcupine has about 30,000 quills each up to 12 cm (5 in) long. Put end to end, they would reach a third of the way up Mount Everest. When attacked, a porcupine charges backwards and sticks its quills into its enemy. As it moves forward again the quills are left behind causing serious wounds.

Amazing But True

A pangolin is covered in very unusual scales because they are actually made from hairs. When a pangolin is born the scales are soft but they soon harden and help to protect the pangolin from predators. Ordinary hair grows between the scales and on the underside of a pangolin's body.

Green hair

The sloth in South America hangs upside-down in trees. Unlike the hair of any other mammmal, a sloth's long hair grows from its stomach down towards its back. Sloths are so dirty that green algae grow on their coats This camouflages the sloth among the trees and is an ideal egg-laying site for some moths. The newly-hatched caterpillars feed on the algae.

Communication

Sights and sounds

Other mammals cannot speak as people do but communicate by smell, sight, sound and touch. Each species has different signals to warn others in the group of danger, mark its territory, call its young or find a mate.

Smelly signals

The tenrec, an insect-eater from Madagascar, spits on a spot it wants to mark, then rubs its hand along its side and on the wet place. It does this to mark its territory with its own strong body smell. Other tenrecs recognise the scent and are warned to stay away.

Tail talk

Dogs use their tails to show their feelings. A happy dog wags its tail. A frightened dog puts its tail between its legs. An angry cat, though, swishes its tail from side to side and holds it upright if it is content.

When two prairie dogs meet they exchange a sort of 'kiss' to find out if they know each other. If they do not, the intruder is driven away but if they do, they 'kiss' again and then start grooming each other. Prairie dog burrows are guarded by sentries who sound the alarm with a series of whistling barks if an enemy is seen.

Baby talk

Baby animals make signals. A baby orang-utan's small size, big eyes, high forehead and jerky movements all give out a special message. They tell the adults in the group that this is a baby who needs to be looked after.

Laughing hyena

Hyenas hunt together in teams and make many different noises for communication. They growl, grunt, whine and yelp but also burst into noisy choruses which sound like hysterical laughter. Only human beings can really laugh.

Body language

Chimpanzees are among the very few mammals which can pull faces to show their feelings. They can show anger, happiness and interest very much like human beings. But if a chimp seems to be grinning, showing its teeth, it is probably frightened, not smiling. Chimps also shake their fists to show anger, and cuddle and touch each other to show affection.

Whale of a song

Whales build up series of sounds into 'songs'. A song may last for about ten minutes but some humpback songs lasting 30 minutes have been recorded. Some are sung over and over again for as long as 24 hours. Whales have very loud voices. Some are even louder than the sound of a jet plane.

Rousing chorus

Howler monkeys live high up in the tree tops in South American forests. To warn off enemies they make one of the loudest mammal sounds. Every morning and evening the monkeys sing in chorus, their throats swelling up like huge balloons. They can be heard about 8 km (5 miles) away.

Amazing But True

Dolphins have a wide vocabulary of over 32 sounds. They use squeals, clicks, barks and whistles to 'talk' to each other. A dolphin uses different sounds to tell others in the group who it is, where it is and to warn them if there is danger. Dolphins also use sound as bats do to navigate and to find their food.

Colour coded

Monkeys have very good eyesight and so can use colour to signal to others in their group or to enemies. Many have brightly-coloured hair and skin which show others which species they belong to and which sex they are.

Mandrill

The male mandrill's scarlet and blue face and bottom warn off rivals.

Uakari

The uakari has a red face which gets brighter if it is angry or excited.

De Brazza's monkey

Moustached monkey

These are part of a large group of monkeys called guenons. Colour is used by the guenons to tell the difference between the many types.

Instinct and intelligence

Clever monkey

Most animals behave according to their instinct but some animals are also able to learn facts and work out problems. Monkeys and apes are among the most intelligent animals. Johnnie, a rhesus monkey living on a farm in Australia, learned to drive a tractor. He was also able to understand commands such as 'turn left' and 'turn right'.

Sign language

A 13-year old gorilla, called Koko, was taught from an early age to use sign language. She now knows about 1,000 words. Koko is very fond of her cat and describes him as 'Soft good cat cat' and herself as 'Fine animal gorilla'. In an intelligence test taken at the age of seven, Koko proved to be just as clever as a human seven-year old.

Some mammals use twigs or stones as tools. The sea otter floats on its back in the water with a large stone balanced on its stomach. It smashes shellfish against the stone to open them up to eat.

The otter keeps its face turned away to avoid being hit by sharp pieces of broken shell. One otter was seen to open 54 mussels in 86 minutes. It smashed them against a stone over 2,000 times.

Washing up

Macaques are very intelligent monkeys. Scientists studying a group of macaques in Japan, began to feed them with sweet potatoes. A year later they were amazed to see a 3½-year old female, Imo, dip her potato in a pool to wash off the sand. The others followed her lead but soon found that washing the food in the sea gave it a better, salty taste.

Going home

Some animals are able to find their way back home even over very long distances. In 1979 a doctor in the USSR found and looked after an injured hedgehog. She later gave it to her granddaughter who lived in another town. Two months later she found the hedgehog sitting on her doorstep again. It had walked 77 km (48 miles) back home, much further than a hedgehog would usually go.

Which way?

In the autumn mammals such as whales and bats make long journeys to warmer places to feed or breed. This is called migration. These animals seem to find their way there and back each year without getting lost. Scientists think they must have a built-in compass telling them which route to take.

Amazing But True

A young artist, D. James Orang, won first prize in an art contest held in 1971 in Kansas, USA. His paintings sold well and he became quite famous. The judges did not realise that the painter was in fact a six-year old orang-utan, Djakarta Jim, living in Topeka Zoo.

More animal nomads

The map shows some of the longest return journeys made by migrating mammals.

⬆ **1** Noctule bat 2,300 km

⬆ **2** European pipistrelle 1,300 km

⬆ **3** Humpback whale 8,000 km

⬆ **4** Alaskan fur seal (male) 5,000 km

⬆ **5** Caribou 2,250 km

Sea marathon

The longest journey is made by grey whales. In late autumn they leave their feeding grounds in the Bering Sea and travel 9,650 km (6,000 miles) south along the west coast of the USA to Mexico. This is about the same distance as from London to Tokyo. In the spring they return north by the same route. The journey takes about 90 days.

Fast asleep

Instinct tells some mammals to hibernate during cold winters when food is scarce. Their breathing and pulse rates slow right down and their body temperature drops. Some live off fat stored in their bodies; others store food in their dens. Marmots hibernate for the longest time. They sleep for 7-8 months every year, losing about a quarter of their body weight.

Families and herds

Safety in numbers

Many mammals live in families or herds. They work together to defend themselves and search for food. Often the members of a group are closely related. A herd of antelopes may include parents and children, aunts, uncles and cousins. Animal groups often have definite leaders.

Job sharing

Mole rats in Africa have very well-organised family groups. One large female is the queen and has all the babies. The smaller mole rats do the hard work, digging tunnels and finding food. The larger rats are much lazier than this. They look after the nests for the young and sound the alarm if they see an intruder near the burrow.

DID YOU KNOW?

The greatest gathering of any one type of mammal takes place on the Pribilof Islands in the Bering Sea. Each year about 1½ million Alaskan fur seals go there to breed, producing 500,000 pups.

Anti-social sloth

Some mammals live very solitary lives. The three-toed sloth spends 18 hours of its day asleep and the rest feeding, all by itself.

Hunting packs

Wolves hunt in packs, following a set plan of attack. When tracking a moose, wolves set out in single file. Once a moose is sighted they stand very still, then suddenly rush towards it. As soon as it starts to run, the wolves attack. A large pack of about 16 wolves may track up to 12 moose before finally catching one.

Amazing But True

Prairie dogs, or ground squirrels, live in vast systems of burrows called 'towns'. Each town is divided into smaller family units called 'coteries'. A prairie dog town found in Texas, USA in the 19th century contained an

incredible 400 million animals. It covered an area about twice the size of Belgium.

The largest herds ever recorded were those of springbok in southern Africa in the 19th century. When food and water became scarce, the springbok would set off in search of new pastures. The last great herd was seen in 1896. It is said to have covered 5,360 sq km (2,070 sq miles), over three times the area of London, England. There were over 10 million animals.

Some animal groups have very unusual names:
A clowder of cats
A leap of leopards
A sloth of bears
A skulk of foxes
A labour of moles
A crash of rhinoceroses
A trip of goats
A shrewdness of apes
A troop of kangaroos
A pride of lions
A pod of dolphins

Bat caves

Bats are very sociable animals and live together in huge cave colonies. The largest bat colony in the world is in Bracken Cave, Texas, USA. During the summer the cave is the home of as many as 20 million Mexican free-tailed bats.

Jumbo care

Elephants live in herds of 200 or more animals, led by female elephants. During the day the herd splits into smaller groups to feed and find water. The young are looked after by one or two mothers in 'nursery' groups. Females spend all their lives with the herd but single males sometimes leave and are then known as 'rogues' because they can become very fierce. If an elephant dies the herd mourns and stays by the body for several days, covering it with leaves and earth before they go away.

Mammals at home

Home, sweet home

The type of home a mammal has depends on how much protection it needs from predators and the weather, and if it needs a safe place for its young. Many mammals do not have fixed homes. They wander in search of food. Some live in one area, called a territory, which they defend against intruders.

Sea mammals have no fixed home in the water but some have special sleeping habits. Florida manatees sleep on the sea bed. They come to the surface every ten minutes or so to breathe. Sea otters sleep floating on the surface. They wind strands of seaweed round their bodies to stop themselves drifting.

Long sleep

Big cats, such as leopards, sleep for between 12-14 hours a day. They lie on the ground or stretch out along tree branches. They do not need shelters as they live in a warm climate and have no natural enemies.

Mouse house

A harvest mouse builds its nest among tall grasses. Large nests are about the size and shape of cricket balls. The mouse splits blades of grass into thin strips with its teeth and weaves them into a framework. The blades are still joined to the stalks so the nest is firmly wedged. The framework is padded out with more grass, feathers and even pieces of string.

Burrows are the most common type of homes for small mammals. Mole rats are among the best burrowers. The Russian mole rat, digging with its teeth, can shift 50 times its own

weight of soil in about 20 minutes. Moles can dig a 2 m (6½ ft) long tunnel in about 12 minutes. At this rate it would take a mole only four years to dig its way from London to Paris.

Apes asleep

Chimpanzees and orang-utans sleep in flimsy, temporary nests up in the trees. It takes a chimp about five minutes to build a nest. It bends branches across to form a firm base and then weaves smaller twigs into it. If the night is cold, apes wrap themselves up in leaf or grass 'blankets'.

Escape routes

Rabbits dig large tunnel systems underground. The tunnels lead to living and sleeping rooms and nurseries. Above ground the rabbits dig out special 'bolt' holes which they stay close to when they are feeding outside. If there is danger, the rabbits bolt head first down the nearest hole to safety underground.

Houseproud badgers

Badgers live in setts made up of chambers with connecting tunnels. One of the largest setts known had 94 tunnels. The same sett may be used over and over again for as long as 250 years. Badgers are very houseproud. They line their bedrooms with bracken, moss and grass. On dry mornings they drag huge piles of bedding outside to air in the sun.

Master builders

Beavers are ingenious builders. First they build a dam of logs and mud across a river to form a pond. In the pond they build a dome-shaped wooden lodge the size of a large tent. With its strong teeth, a beaver can fell a tree ½ m (20 in) thick in just 15 minutes. Inside the lodge is a living area above water level, reached through underwater tunnels.

Record breaker

Beaver dams are usually about 23 m (75 ft) long. The largest dam ever built is on the Jefferson River, USA. It is 700 m (2,296 ft) long and strong enough to bear the weight of a person riding across it on horseback.

Bear caves

Some bears hibernate in the winter when it is cold and food is scarce. They dig dens in the ground or find caves or hollow trees to live in. A female polar bear digs a den in the snow in October and has her cubs there. They leave the den in the spring.

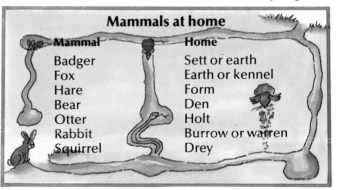

Mammals at home

Mammal	Home
Badger	Sett or earth
Fox	Earth or kennel
Hare	Form
Bear	Den
Otter	Holt
Rabbit	Burrow or warren
Squirrel	Drey

Runners

Fastest on land

Cheetahs are the fastest land mammals with a top speed of 115 kph (71 mph), as fast as an average car. They can only run fast for short distances though and have to rest after about 500 m (550 yards). Cheetahs have flexible backbones which allow

them to take giant 7 m (23 ft) leaps. They can reach 72 kph (45 mph) from a standstill in just two seconds. In the 1930s cheetahs were raced against greyhounds in London. The cheetahs won.

Let's dance

Sifakas, or white lemurs, of Madagascar spend a lot of their time high up in the tree tops. They can swing easily from tree to tree. Their legs are much longer than their 'arms' so running on all fours along the ground is impossible. Instead, they do a type of dance on their back legs. They bounce from one foot to the other, holding their arms high in the air.

Pronghorn puff

The fastest land mammal over long distances is the pronghorn antelope of the USA. It can keep up a speed of 45-50 kph (28-31 mph) for about 14 minutes and has a top speed of 85 kph (53 mph). A pronghorn can run fast for so long because it has very well-developed lungs and a heart twice as big as that of other animals of a similar size.

DID YOU KNOW?

The sloth is the slowest land mammal in the world with a top speed of only 2 kph (1.3 mph). It would take a sloth travelling at normal speed about 22 minutes to go 100 m (110 yards). The fastest man in the world can run this distance in under 10 seconds.

Top speeds

Cheetah	115 kph
Blackbuck	80 kph
Brown hare	72 kph
Race horse	69 kph
Greyhound	66 kph
Red fox	64 kph
Giraffe	51 kph
African elephant	40 kph
Arabian camel	32 kph
American porcupine	16 kph
House rat	9 kph
Common shrew	4 kph
Sloth	2 kph

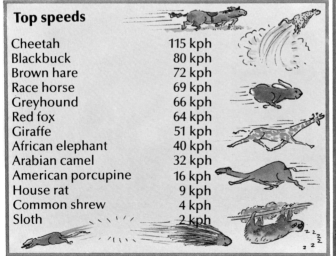

Climbers

Climbing aid

Some mammals have their own special ways of making climbing up tree trunks easier. The slow-moving Canadian porcupine has non-slip pads on the soles of its feet. It also has spines underneath its tail which help it to grip the tree trunk. An African spiny squirrel also has spines on its tail.

Sure-footed

Some mammals have specially adapted feet for climbing. Rocky Mountain goats in the USA are very sure-footed and can climb up nearly vertical slopes and walk safely along narrow ledges. Their hooves have sharp edges which dig into cracks in the rocks to give a secure foothold and their soles have hollows which stick to rocks like suction pads.

Amazing But True

One of the best mountain climbers was a beagle from Switzerland called Tschingel. From 1868-1876 she climbed 53 of the most difficult mountains in the Alps, 11 of which had never been climbed before, and many easier ones. In 1875 she climbed Mont Blanc, the highest mountain in the Alps and was made a member of the exclusive Alpine Club.

Short cut

Most big cats are good climbers but the puma has an easier way of getting up and down trees. It is an excellent jumper. From a standstill it can leap 7 m (23 ft) up into a tree and jump down to the ground from heights of up to 18 m (60 ft).

Speedy climber

The fastest animal mountain climber is the chamois, a mountain goat which lives in the Pyrenees and Alps in Europe. It can climb 1,000 m (3,280 ft) in only 15 minutes. At this rate a chamois could climb to the top of Mount Everest, the highest point on Earth, in just over two hours.

Swinging gibbons

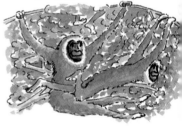

Some mammals do not need to climb well. A gibbon has arms twice as long as its body. The easiest way for it to move through the trees is to swing. Its armspan is about 2.1 m (7ft) and it can swing 12 m (39 ft) from one branch to the next, gripping the branches firmly with its long, curved fingers.

27

Flying mammals

Air-borne bats

Bats are the only mammals which can fly although some mammals can glide. There are over 900 different species. Bats are the second largest group of mammals, after rodents and make up one fifth of the world's mammals. Bats live all over the world, except in very cold places. There are two main groups – the large fruit bats or flying foxes, and the smaller insect-eaters. Some bats also feed on birds, lizards, fish, nectar and blood.

Nectar eaters

Jamaican flower bats and tube-nosed fruit bats eat nectar. They hover near flowers and stick their long tongues deep down inside to reach the food. Bats help to pollinate flowers. Pollen stuck to their bodies is carried to another flower.

Taking to the air

The Latin word for bats is 'chiroptera' which means 'hand-wings'. About 60 million years ago some insect-eating mammals developed into bats and their bodies became adapted for flight. A bat's wings have formed from its hands and arms. Its fingers are very long and support the skin stretched across them. The thumb is left free. The wing is also attached to the bat's back legs and often to its tail.

DID YOU KNOW?

Vampires are the most dangerous bats as they spread diseases such as rabies. There are many legends about vampires. In Eastern Europe it was thought that vampires were evil people who could turn into bats. To gain control over other people, they sucked their blood. Some ways of scaring away vampires were to show them a crucifix or to wear a necklace of garlic.

Bat ears

Bats have the best hearing of all land mammals. They have very sensitive and often very large ears which some use for locating their prey in the dark. The long-eared bat's body is only 5 cm (2 in) long but its ears are 4 cm (1½ in) long. If the bat was as big as a hare, its ears would be over 44 cm (1½ ft) long.

Bat homes

Bat facts

Largest	Bismarck flying fox
Smallest	Bumblebee bat
Most common	Typical small bats (pipistrelle; noctule bats)
Fastest flying	Brazilian free-tailed bat
Average life span	10-20 years
Average young	One baby or twins

Bats feed at night and spend the day sleeping in caves or in tree tops. Some caves may be home to thousands of bats. Other bats make temporary shelters. They sleep under banana leaves, in empty burrows or even inside bamboo stems. Some South American bats make tent-like shelters out of palm tree leaves.

Catching fish

The hare-lipped bat in tropical America is an expert fisherman. It flies low over ponds and lakes. Spotting a fish just below the surface, it swoops down, raking the water with its large claws and scoops the fish up into its mouth. Its legs are not attached to the skin of its wings so they are free to act as fish hooks.

Winter warmth

To avoid the cold winter months, some bats migrate to warmer places. Noctule bats travel the furthest, flying 2,300 km (1,430 miles) from Moscow to Bulgaria. Other bats hibernate in caves or in hollow tree trunks. Most hibernating mammals wake up every 10-20 days but brown bats sleep solidly for up to 66 days.

Flying lemurs

A few mammals are very good gliders though they cannot actually fly. Flying lemurs, or colugos, of the Far East are about the size of rabbits. Their front and back legs are joined by folds of furry skin down each side. The colugo spreads these out like wings and glides from tree to tree. It can glide for a distance of 91 m (300 ft) before landing.

Super gliders

Flying phalangers, such as the sugar glider, of Australia, and the flying squirrels of North America can also glide from tree to tree. Flying phalangers are in fact marsupials. They glide with their young in their pouches until the babies are two months old. Flying squirrels are rodents. They can glide as far as 450 m (⅓ mile).

Sea mammals

Sea mammals

There are over 4,000 species of mammals but only about 121 of these are sea mammals. Sea mammals are divided into three groups:

Pinnipedes – seals, sea-lions, walruses (32 species)

Sirenians (or sea cows) – manatees, dugongs (4 species)

Cetaceans – whales, dolphins, porpoises (about 85 species)

Sea unicorn

A narwhal has only two teeth which grow straight forward from its top jaw. The male's left tooth carries on growing in a spiral. It can be up to 2.5 m (9 ft) long. Narwhals are nearly extinct today because they were once hunted for their valuable tusks which were sold as unicorn horns. No one has yet found out what narwhals use their tusks for.

DID YOU KNOW?

The ancestors of sea mammals once lived on land. About 50 million years ago they began to return to the sea for food and their bodies adapted to life in the water. The whale's front legs became flippers, its back legs disappeared

and its nostrils became a blow-hole on top of its head. Sea mammals can hold their breath for a long time. A fin-back whale is able to stay underwater for 40 minutes; a bottle-nosed dolphin for two hours.

Seal tears

Seals lying on rocks out of the water often look as if they are crying. This is because they produce tears to keep their eyes moist. In the sea the tears get washed away but on land they trickle down the seals' cheeks.

Humpback acrobat

The humpback is the most athletic whale. It leaps high into the air and crashes down into the water on its back. It can even turn complete somersaults in the air. A humpback whale's body is often covered in barnacles which may weigh as much as eight people. The whale may leap to try and get rid of the weight.

Power propeller

The killer whale is the fastest sea mammal. It uses its strong tail as a propeller to speed it through the water. Thrashing its tail up and down, it can reach a top speed of about 65 kph (40 mph), eight times faster than the fastest human swimmer.

Whale blubber

Instead of fur, whales have a thick layer of fat, called blubber, round their bodies. Blubber keeps them warm and helps support their large bodies in the water. Some whales have blubber 38 cm (15 in) thick. Whales have long been hunted for the valuable oils in their blubber. A blue whale's blubber can weigh as much as four tractors and may contain over 120 barrels of oil.

Pinnipede records

Largest	Southern elephant seal
Smallest	Ringed seal
Fastest	Californian sea-lion
Deepest-diver	Weddell seal
Most common	Crabeater seal
Rarest	Monk seal

Amazing But True

The mermaid legend is thought to come from the rather ugly dugong. Close to, it is hard to believe that these lumbering creatures could have been mistaken for mermaids but from a distance they do look a little like human forms with fish-like tails.

Dolphin care

Some dolphins travel in family groups called pods, of up to 1,000 animals. If a dolphin is ill or wounded, the others push it to the surface so it can still breathe. A shark may be able to kill a single dolphin but if it attacks a pod, the dolphins ram it with their 'beaks'. They scare the shark off and may even kill it.

Walking teeth

In the breeding season huge herds of walruses gather on islands in the Bering Sea. Adults, which can weigh over a tonne, use their tusks to drag themselves over the land. The Latin name for walrus, *Odobenus rosmarus*, actually means 'the one who walks with its teeth'.

Mammals of the cold

Out in the cold

Mammals living in very cold places need special survival skills. Many have thick coats for keeping warm and broad feet for walking on ice and snow. The vicuña, a relation of the camel, lives in the Andes in South America. It has such a warm coat that it can even overheat. But it also has bare patches on its legs. To cool down, it turns so that these are facing the wind.

High home

The highest-living mammal is the wild yak of Tibet and China. It can climb to heights of over 6,000 m (20,000 ft) in search of food. Its long, thick blackish coat protects it from the biting cold. People in Nepal keep domestic yaks for milk, wool and dung for fuel.

Snowshoe rabbit

Snowshoe rabbits in North America get their name from their broad feet. These act like snowshoes and stop the rabbit sinking in the deep snow. Long hairs grow on the sides of the feet and between the toes. They keep the rabbit's feet warm and help them to grip the frozen ground.

DID YOU KNOW?

Macaques living high up in the mountains of northern Japan have to cope with very harsh winters. They keep warm by taking long baths in the hot, volcanic springs nearby.

Cool cats

The rare snow leopard, or ounce, lives in the mountains of Central Asia. It has a thick, smoky-grey coat with black rosette markings. In summer the snow leopard lives nearly 6,000 m (20,000 ft) up in the mountain peaks. In winter it comes down to the lower slopes below 3,000 m (10,000 ft) in search of food.

All change

The Arctic fox, some stoats and the snow hare change colour as the seasons change. They have brown summer coats, moult in autumn and turn white in winter. Throughout the year they blend in with the countryside and are very well hidden from hungry predators.

Mountain mammals

The list shows the maximum heights at which various mammals are found.

By comparison, Mount Everest, the highest point on Earth, is 8,848 m tall.

- Tibetan antelope
- 6,000 m Woolly hare
- 5,800 m Mongolian wolf
- 5,600 m Puma
- 5,500 m Brown bear
- 4,700 m Snow vole
- 3,600 m Red panda

Abominable snowman

Many people claim to have seen yetis in the Himalayas. They are supposed to be ape-like creatures with long, shaggy coats. In 1951 photographs of yeti footprints were published but no one has proved yetis exist. It is thought that yetis are, in fact, large black or brown bears. A more unusual explanation is that they are 'visions' or hallucinations caused by a lack of oxygen at high altitudes.

Deep-sea diver

The Weddell seal lives in the Antarctic, further south than any other mammal. It spends most of its time under the pack ice, kept warm by a thick layer of fat under its skin. It chews holes in the ice to reach air to breathe.

Hardy huskies

Husky dogs are among the hardiest animals. They have thick coats and can live in temperatures as low as −45°C (−50°F) without shelter. They are also very strong. A team of 12 can pull a sled weighing half a tonne, as much as eight people and their luggage.

Amazing But True

Polar bears are sometimes seen on land. A teacher at a school near the northerly Kara Sea, USSR, heard the door bell ring and went to answer it. She found that the caller was a huge polar bear leaning on the door bell.

Ice bear

The largest polar mammal is the polar bear. The heaviest recorded weighed over a tonne. Polar bears live on the pack ice near the North Pole. This is the bear's hunting ground. It waits by an air-hole for a seal to surface and kills it with a blow of its paw. Polar bears are strong swimmers but prefer to use pieces of ice as rafts.

Mammals of the desert

Desert life

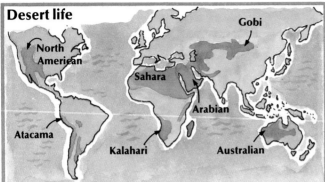

Deserts have less than 25 cm (10 in) of rain a year. They cover about a fifth of the Earth's land surface. Deserts are sandy, rocky or covered in stones and gravel. The Sahara Desert is almost as big as the whole USA. The temperature there may reach 57°C (134°F) during the day and drop well below freezing at night. Many plants and animals live in deserts. They all face the same problem – finding enough water to stay alive.

Plant food

Desert plants provide food and water for many animals. Cacti store water in their leaves and stems. Giant saguaro cacti in the North American deserts can weigh as much as 10 tonnes of which 9 tonnes may be water. Mammals eat the plants and seeds and can get enough water from them to live without drinking.

Underground cool

Most small desert mammals spend the day underground to avoid the heat. Scientists studying gerbil burrows in the Kara-Kum Desert, USSR, found that just 10 cm (4 in) below ground the temperature was 17°C (61°F) cooler than above. Mammals' breathing helps keep the burrows moist. In the day the burrow entrance is blocked to stop moisture escaping.

Sand survivor

The rare addax, a type of antelope, lives among the sanddunes in the southern Sahara. It is one of the few large mammals that can survive such harsh conditions. The addax never needs to drink. It gets all its moisture from the plants it eats.

DID YOU KNOW?

About 5,000 years ago the Sahara Desert was covered in rich grassland and trees. Paintings found in caves in Tassili, Algeria, which date from about that time, show giraffe, hippopotamus and lions, people hunting and cattle grazing.

Living in the desert

Here are some of the ways mammals have of coping with the desert heat and lack of water:

1 Hunt only during cooler night
2 Sweat very little so lose little water
3 Get water from the plants and seeds they eat
4 Concentrated urine so body loses less water
5 Large ears which give off excess heat
6 Small mammals spend day in cool burrows

Kit fox

The kit fox hunts for food at night, well hidden by its greyish-black coat. It has excellent hearing for detecting its prey in the dark. It also loses heat through its large ears to keep cool and they are lined with thick hair to keep out dust and sand.

Spit and polish

Desert wallabies and kangaroos in Australia have an unusual way of keeping cool. When it gets very hot they pant and make a lot of saliva. They lick the saliva over their bodies and rub their faces with their wet paws.

Little leaper

Kangaroo rats are an important part of desert life. They are often eaten by other animals for the water in their bodies. The rats can hop very fast to avoid their enemies, covering 6 m (20 ft) in one second. They use their long tails as rudders when jumping and can even change their course in mid-air.

Sleepy squirrel

The Mojave squirrel in the USA survives long droughts by sleeping for whole days at a time in its underground burrow. Sleeping through hot, dry weather is called aestivation. The squirrel saves energy and is out of the heat.

Ships of the desert

There are two types of camel – the one-humped Arabian camel and the two-humped Bactrian camel. Both are well equipped for desert life. A camel's hump can weigh up to 13.5 kg (30 lb) and contains fat which can be used when there is no food. Camels can survive for many days without food and water. After a drought they will drink up to 114 litres (25 gallons) of water in one go.

Worlds apart

Australia's animals

Because Australia has been cut off from the rest of the world for over 60 million years, it has very unusual animals. Almost all its mammals are marsupials (mammals with pouches). There are over 150 kinds of Australian marsupials from tiny marsupial mice and moles to marsupial cats. Outside Australia marsupials are only found in South America with just one species in North America.

Honey possum

A honey possum, or noolbenger, of Western Australia, is about the size of a mouse. It has a special way of eating nectar and pollen. Its long tongue is covered in bristles with a tip like a tiny brush. Pollen sticks to the brush as it feeds.

Some unusual marsupials

Boodie

Member of the rat kangaroo family.

Numbat

Also called a banded anteater.

Quoll

A marsupial cat.

Bandicoot

Pouch opens to rear. Latin name means 'badger with a pouch'.

Amazing But True

The biggest collection of marsupial fossils was found in the Naracoorte Caves, Australia, in 1969. They showed giant marsupials including a creature the size of a rhinoceros. It probably died out about 40,000 years ago.

Wombat digger

Wombats are about the same size and shape as badgers. They are expert diggers and live in huge underground burrows surrounded by a maze of tunnels. A wombat's pouch opens backwards so that the baby being carried inside is not showered with earth as the wombat digs.

Marsupial records

Biggest	Red kangaroo	Up to 2.13 m tall
Smallest	Ingram's planigale	9 cm long
Fastest	Red kangaroo	48 kph
Rarest	Marsupial wolf	Last known died 1933.
Most common	Kangaroo	Over 50 species
Longest-lived	Common wombat	26 years

Madagascar

Madagascar is a huge island off the east coast of Africa. It is bigger than France. About 30 million years ago it became separated from Africa. Nine-tenths of the island's animals and plants are found nowhere else in the world. Its most famous mammals are lemurs which are related to monkeys and apes.

DID YOU KNOW?

The sportive lemur gets its name because, if attacked, it raises its fists like a boxer and punches its enemy. It feeds on Somy tree flowers. The tree is covered in sharp spikes but the lemur does not seem to hurt itself as it leaps from stem to stem.

Rousing chorus

The indri, the largest of the lemurs, lives mostly high up in the tree tops. It uses sound to scare away enemies and call its young. Every morning and evening, families of indris break into wailing songs. Each indri joins in at a different time so the strange chorus may last for many minutes.

Sun worship

Sifakas, or white lemurs, start off each day by lying in the sun for an hour or so. They climb to a tree top and face the sun with their arms outstretched. They do this to warm themselves up after a cool night but local people believed that the lemurs were worshipping the sun.

Fat store

Dwarf lemurs are amongst the smallest of the lemurs. The fat-tailed dwarf lemur eats insects, leaves and sap. During the rainy season it builds up a fat store under its skin and in its tail. It lives off this supply in the dry season when food is scarce.

Tenrecs

Another group of mammals found only in Madagascar are tenrecs. There are about 20 species of these small insect-eaters. Some have bristly coats like hedgehogs, others have fur. The common tenrec is the largest insect-eater in Madagascar. It may be as much as 40 cm (16 in) long, about the same size as a cat.

Mammals in danger

Under threat

Over 550 species of mammals are in danger of dying out for ever. When an animal species dies out, it is said to be extinct. If it is likely to die out unless it is protected, it is said to be endangered or threatened.

Why in danger

Many mammals become endangered because their homes are destroyed by farmers or foresters or they are hunted for their meat or fur. The South American rain forests contain about half of the world's plant and animal species. As they are destroyed to make room for farms or buildings, thousands of species are lost. It is thought that a piece of rain forest the size of Switzerland is cut down each year.

Run, rhino, run

All five species of rhinoceros are listed as endangered. Rhinos have long been hunted for their horns. A powder made from horn was thought to cure fevers and headaches. In 1978 there were about 140,000 rhino in the wild. Ten years later this number had been reduced to 14,000.

Giant panda

Giant pandas once lived all over China but are now only found in the south-west. Pandas live mainly on bamboo. If this dies or is cut down, they may starve. In 1981 the World Wildlife Fund and the Chinese Government started the project 'Save the Panda' to protect them.

DID YOU KNOW?

In 1700 there were some 60 million buffalo in North America. Millions were killed for their meat and because their grazing land was needed for farming. By 1880 there were only a few hundred left. Today the buffalo are making a slow comeback. There are now about 10,000 in the wild.

Operation tiger

Many of the big cats, including the Asian lion, the leopard and the tiger, are endangered. In 1945 there were over 100,000 tigers in India; by 1970 probably about 4,000 were left. Tigers were hunted for their fur and for sport. Today there are special tiger reserves in India and tigers are now strictly protected by law.

Monkeys and apes

The golden lion tamarin is one of the world's rarest monkeys. Only about 200 still survive in patches of forest in Brazil. Much of the monkey's forest home has been cleared to make way for sugar cane and coffee plantations and for building. One fifth of all the species of monkeys and apes in the world are endangered, including proboscis monkeys, black gibbons, chimpanzees and orang-utans.

Some endangered mammals

Mountain gorilla (Africa)	Less than 400 left in the wild.
Arabian oryx	Last seen in the wild in 1972. Now being re-introduced.
Indian lion	Hunted and forest home destroyed.
African elephant	Over 50,000 killed a year for the ivory from their tusks.
Grey whale (North Pacific)	Migration routes and breeding grounds destroyed by ships.
Baiji dolphin (China)	Less than 400 left; the most threatened whale species.
Sea otter (North Pacific)	Hunted for valuable fur; hunting now banned.

How to help

Unless human beings stop destroying habitats and polluting water, mammals such as blue whales and polar bears could become extinct by the beginning of the next century. The World Wildlife Fund was set up in 1961 to help protect the world's animals. It now has over 4,000 conservation projects in over 135 countries round the world. Groups like this and laws banning hunting or poaching have helped save some of the mammals most at risk.

Unsafe seas

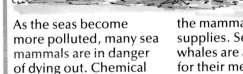

As the seas become more polluted, many sea mammals are in danger of dying out. Chemical waste, sewage and oil spilt from tankers kill the mammals' food supplies. Seals and whales are also hunted for their meat and skins. Today they are protected but some are still killed.

It is thought that there are now only 500 Mediterranean monk seals left and that the Caribbean monk seal may be extinct.

The smallest mammals

Smallest on land

The smallest land mammal is the tiny Savi's pygmy shrew which lives in southern Europe and Africa. It is 3.8 cm (1½ in) long with a tail which measures 2.5 cm (1 in). A fully-grown shrew weighs only about as much as a table tennis ball.

Smallest meat eater

The dwarf or least weasel which lives in Siberia is the smallest carnivore. An adult measures 17-20 cm (6.6-7.8 in) in length. It weighs about as much as ten lumps of sugar.

Pencil legs

The royal antelope which lives in West Africa is the smallest antelope in the world. Adults are only 25-30 cm (10-12 in) tall and weigh about 3-3.6 kg (7-8 lb). A royal antelope living in the London Zoo was said to have had legs thinner than pencils. Its hooves were so tiny that it was able to stand in a teaspoon with room to spare.

DID YOU KNOW?

The very rare bumblebee bat from Thailand is the smallest flying mammal. Adults have a wingspan of about 160 mm (6.3 in), about the same as that of a large butterfly. They weigh about as much as five drawing pins.

Smallest at sea

The smallest mammal in the seas is the Commerson's dolphin. An adult weighs 25-35 kg (55-77 lb), 3,500 times lighter than a blue whale, the largest sea mammal.

Miniature monkeys

The world's smallest primate is the lesser mouse lemur which lives on the island of Madagascar. When it is fully grown, it is about 11 cm (4.3 in) long, with a 15 cm (6 in) long tail. It

weighs only 50 g (1.7 oz). The tiny pygmy marmoset which lives in South America comes a close second. It weighs up to 75 g (2.6 oz), about as much as a hen's egg.

More small fry

Group	Smallest	Average weight (adult male)
Cat family	Rusty-spotted cat	1.35 kg
Seals	Ringed seal	127 kg
Deer	Northern pudu	7-8 g
Rodents	Northern pygmy mouse	7-8 kg
Domestic cat	Singapura	1.8 kg
Freshwater mammal	Southern water shrew	7.5-16 g
Bears	Malay bear	25-40 kg

Pocket sized

The very rare Ingram's planigale, a type of pouched mouse found only in north-west Australia, is the smallest marsupial in the world. Its body and head are 45 mm (1.7 in) long, its tail the same length again and it weighs only a little more than an airmail envelope.

The smallest dogs

The smallest breed of dogs is the chihuahua but the smallest dog ever known was a Yorkshire terrier. It died in 1945 aged two years. It was 6.3 cm (2½ in) tall at the shoulder, only 9.5 cm (3¾ in) from its nose to its tail and weighed an incredible 113 g (4 oz), about the same size as a hamster.

Mini horse

The smallest breed of horse is the Falabella from Argentina. Adults are less than 76 cm (30 in) tall. The smallest horse ever known was a tiny stallion called Little Pumpkin from the USA. Fully grown, it was only about the size of a small dog.

Amazing But True

The closest relation to the African elephant, the world's largest living land mammal, is said to be the comparatively tiny hyrax. Hyraxes are about the size of rabbits but in prehistoric times they were almost as large as cows. Elephants and hyraxes are thought to have come from the same group of mammals, millions of years ago.

41

The biggest mammals

Sea giant

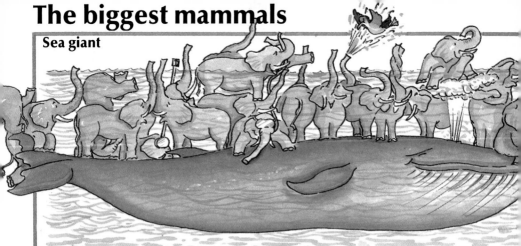

The biggest mammal that has ever lived is the gigantic blue whale. A female caught in the South Atlantic in 1922 was over 33 m (110 ft) long, nearly 1½ times as long as an Olympic swimming pool. Blue whales are also the heaviest mammals in the world. A single whale can weigh as much as 130 tonnes, over 20 times heavier than a bull (male) African elephant and almost as heavy as 2,000 men.

Amazing But True

A blue whale calf is the biggest mammal baby. When it is born, a calf can be over 7 m (25 ft) long and weigh nearly 2 tonnes. By drinking up to 600 litres (132 gallons) of its mother's rich milk a day it can double its weight in just a week. By the time it is seven months old, a calf may weigh as much as 23 tonnes.

Largest on land

The biggest land mammal in the world is the African elephant. An adult bull (male) is usually about 3 m (10½ ft) tall and weighs some 5½ tonnes. The largest African elephant ever recorded was about 4 m (13 ft) tall and weighed over 12 tonnes, as much as 16 average-sized cars.

Skyscraper

With its long neck and legs, the giraffe is the tallest mammal on Earth. An adult Masai giraffe bull can be over 5 m (17 ft) tall. A tall man would only come up to the top of its leg. The tallest giraffe ever recorded in the world was 5.87 m (19 ft 3 in) tall.

Gentle giant

The largest ape is the mountain gorilla in Africa. An average male stands 1.75 m (5 ft 9 in) tall and weighs about 195 kg (430 lb), with a massive chest of 1.5 m (5 ft). Gorillas are very gentle but very strong. Scientists have worked out that a two-year old gorilla's arms are about three times stronger than a two-year old child's.

Wonder wings

The largest flying mammal is the Bismarck flying fox, a bat from New Guinea. Its head and body are only 45 cm (18 in) long, but it can measure 1.6 m (5½ ft) across its outstretched wings, 2½ times the wingspan of a pigeon.

DID YOU KNOW?

The sperm whale has the heaviest mammal brain. Its brain weighs up to 9 kg (20 lb), six times heavier than a human brain. The whale has a very large head, about a third of its body length, so there is plenty of room for its big brain.

Biggest rodent

The capybara in South America is the world's largest rodent. It is about the size of a sheep, weighing up to 113 kg (250 lb). A harvest mouse, one of the smallest rodents in the world, is over 18,000 times lighter than its heavyweight relation.

Heavyweights

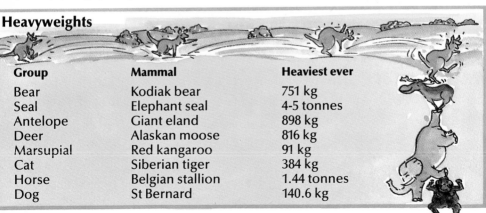

Group	Mammal	Heaviest ever
Bear	Kodiak bear	751 kg
Seal	Elephant seal	4-5 tonnes
Antelope	Giant eland	898 kg
Deer	Alaskan moose	816 kg
Marsupial	Red kangaroo	91 kg
Cat	Siberian tiger	384 kg
Horse	Belgian stallion	1.44 tonnes
Dog	St Bernard	140.6 kg

Habitat map

The type of place a mammal lives in is called its habitat. The larger map shows six main habitats and some of the animals found in them.

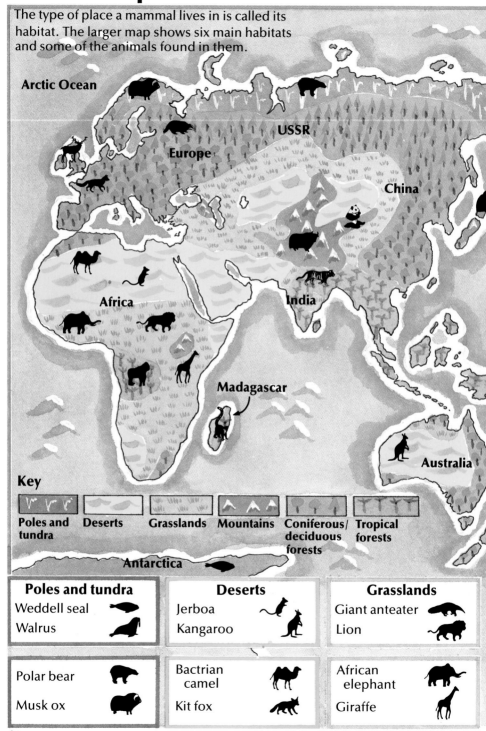

Arctic Ocean

USSR

Europe

China

Africa

India

Madagascar

Australia

Antarctica

Key

Poles and tundra | Deserts | Grasslands | Mountains | Coniferous/ deciduous forests | Tropical forests

Poles and tundra

Weddell seal

Walrus

Polar bear

Musk ox

Deserts

Jerboa

Kangaroo

Bactrian camel

Kit fox

Grasslands

Giant anteater

Lion

African elephant

Giraffe

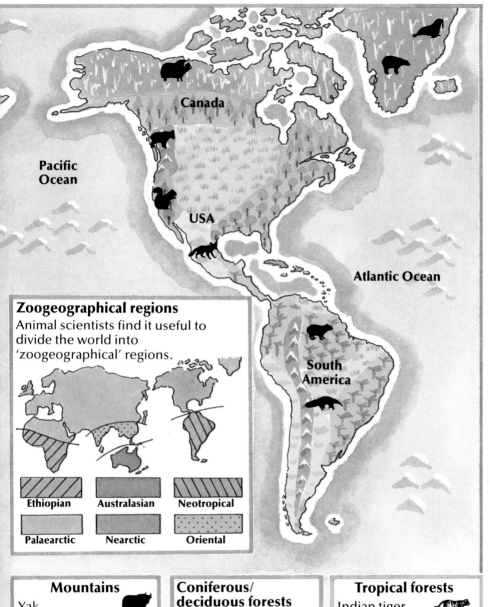

Canada

Pacific Ocean

USA

Atlantic Ocean

South America

Zoogeographical regions

Animal scientists find it useful to divide the world into 'zoogeographical' regions.

Ethiopian

Australasian

Neotropical

Palaearctic

Nearctic

Oriental

Mountains	
Yak	
Giant panda	

Japanese macaque	
Mountain goat	

Coniferous/ deciduous forests	
Red deer	

Grey squirrel	
Red fox	
European badger	

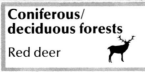

Tropical forests	
Indian tiger	
Capybara	

Gorilla	
Ring-tailed lemur	

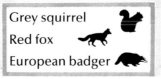

Glossary

Adaptation Special characteristics to help animals survive. For example, Arctic mammals have very thick, warm fur to protect them from the cold.

Aestivation A time of inactivity or deep sleep to save energy and keep cool during very hot and dry weather.

Camouflage Some mammals have special colouring or markings which help disguise them and hide them from their enemies.

Carnivore An animal that only or mainly eats meat.

Conservation Protecting rare animals from becoming extinct.

Endangered Animals in danger of becoming extinct or dying out.

Evolution Animals gradually change over a very long time to become better suited to the way in which they live (depending on food supplies, habitat and climate).

Extinct Animals that no longer exist. They become officially extinct if there have been no certain records of them for 50 years.

Gestation The length of time of a mammal's pregnancy.

Habitat The type of place an animal lives in, for example, desert, jungle, mountain, grassland.

Herbivore An animal such as an elephant that mostly or only eats plants.

Hibernation A deep sleep or time of inactivity to save energy during the cold, winter months.

Marsupial Mammals with pouches. Their young are born tiny and ill-formed. They feed and grow further inside their mother's pouch.

Migration A return journey made by some mammals every year to a place for feeding or breeding.

Monotreme A mammal which lays eggs such as the duck-billed platypus and spiny anteater. The most primitive group of mammals.

Nocturnal Animals such as bats that are active at night when they hunt for food and rest during the day.

Omnivore Animals that eat both plants and meat.

Placental mammal The young develop fully inside the mother's body before they are born.

Predator A hunting animal that kills other animals for food.

Primates The group of mammals that includes monkeys, apes and man. Their special features include a large brain, and fingers (and sometimes toes) designed for grasping.

Territory An area which an animal or group of animals 'owns' and defends against other animals.

Vertebrate An animal with a backbone and an internal skeleton. Fish, amphibians, reptiles, birds and mammals are all vertebrates.

Warm-blooded Animals that can control their own body temperature so it stays the same whatever the weather outside, allowing them to be active in the heat or cold.

Index